Original title:
Fir Friends Forever

Copyright © 2025 Creative Arts Management OÜ
All rights reserved.

Author: Sophia Kingsley
ISBN HARDBACK: 978-1-80567-309-5
ISBN PAPERBACK: 978-1-80567-608-9

Echoes of Shared Journeys

We wandered through the trees so tall,
Tripped on roots and made a call.
Laughed so hard, we lost our breath,
A raccoon stole our snacks; oh, death!

Starlit Gatherings in the Clearing

Beneath the stars we made our pact,
To scare the fireflies with a dance so whacked.
The moon's our witness, oh what a sight,
With giggles echoing through the night.

Nature's Gentle Embrace

Squirrels chattered, trying to tease,
As we crafted crowns made of leaves with ease.
Thought we were wise, but oh what a jest,
Two tangled in vines, a nature fest!

Guardians of the Woodland

In capes of moss, we took our stand,
Defending the forest with the silliest band.
Our battle cries were nothing but giggles,
As we chased each other, doing funny wiggles!

A Journey of Roots and Rays

In the park we play and shout,
With giggles that bounce around,
Chasing squirrels, oh, what a rout,
On the ground we roll and bound.

Wobbly bikes and ice cream drips,
Laughter spills from every face,
We take wild, silly trips,
With no need for any grace.

We share secrets, silly dreams,
Under trees that sway and sway,
Splitting up the chocolate creams,
As the sun begins to play.

At twilight's glow, we make a pact,
With shadows dancing in the breeze,
To stick together, that's a fact,
With laughter hanging from the trees.

The Ties that Bind

In a glade where laughter rings,
The squirrels play, while a bird sings.
Branches swing, a playful dance,
Rooted strong, in a silly prance.

Twisted trunks and knotted vines,
Tell secrets like olden signs.
With every rustle, a joke's on cue,
Nature's humor, all for you.

A Forest Full of Dreams

In the woods, dreams skitter by,
Under leaves, they jump and fly.
Raccoons wearing hats, oh so grand,
Sipping tea from cups they'd planned.

Beneath the boughs, a rabbit scoffs,
While wise old owls giggle and coughs.
Every critter, a tale to spin,
In this dreamland, we all win.

Stories Under the Stars

Gather 'round, the night is bright,
Chirping crickets, what a sight!
Frogs tell tales, so wild and free,
While fireflies dance, oh can't you see?

The moon's a grin, so wide and round,
Whispering secrets of the ground.
With every blink, a story's told,
In the forest, it never gets old.

The Ever-Expanding Canopy

Branches stretch like arms in cheer,
Leaves waving, drawing near.
A canopy of giggles and glee,
Where every critter climbs a tree.

Beneath this roof, friendships bloom,
With a raccoon's hat and a playful broom.
In this green realm, shadows dance,
Growing fonder with each glance.

Branches That Intertwine

In a park where squirrels play,
Two trees chat in their own way.
One says, 'I had a rough day,
Birds keep stealing my green bouquet.'

The other laughs and swings a limb,
'Don't fret, my friend, just live and grin!
Join me for a breeze, a leafy swim,
We'll dance till the sky grows dim.'

A Tapestry of Green

Lush and bright, the leaves do sway,
Gather 'round to share the play.
Worms and bugs all join the fray,
   Creating mishaps every day!

Caterpillars munching leaves at will,
Laugh so hard, they start to spill.
'Who knew being green could be such a thrill?
Join me, pals, let's climb a hill!'

Seasons of Togetherness

When winter comes with chilly breath,
We bundle up, defying death.
Sipping sap through frozen net,
Giggles echo; no need for a bet!

Spring brings blooms and pollen too,
Sneezing loudly, one friend flew!
Hop and skip, we dance in dew,
Planting jokes—it's our debut!

The Canopy of Companionship

Under the shade, we spy a bee,
Zooming past as fast as can be.
'Excuse me, folks, don't bother me!'
Laughing till we all agree!

Friends like us grow wide and tall,
With laughter weaving through it all.
In this forest, we're having a ball,
Together we stand, and never fall!

Moments in the Shade

Squirrels chatter, tails a-sway,
Under branches where we play.
Nutty jokes and acorn cheers,
Laughter echoes through the years.

Sunlight filters, dappled gold,
Stories shared, all tales retold.
Tickles from the playful breeze,
Rustling leaves bring us to ease.

Here we dance, a wobbly jig,
Rolling round, oh what a gig!
With every tree, a silly song,
In our shade, we all belong.

Embrace of the Needles

Prickly hugs from needles green,
Soft and cozy, like a dream.
We gather close, in whispers share,
Giggles float upon the air.

With every branch, a silly tale,
Funky hats, we never fail.
Pinecone games and jumping high,
Tickle fights under the sky.

Mushrooms dance, so weird yet neat,
Bowling balls of pine and peat.
Nature's laughter, wild and free,
Comes alive in our old tree.

Harmony Among the Branches

Chirping birds join in our fun,
Swinging branches, game begun.
Bouncing balls of leaves and laughter,
In our hearts, the joy thereafter.

Whisker-twitch of furry friends,
Racing till the fun finally ends.
Rolling down a hill of jays,
Finding zest in silly ways.

Drawing circles in the dirt,
Hats made funny, never hurt.
Every gust a giggly cheer,
Nature's jesters gather here.

The Forest's Embrace

Tickling wind through roots and pine,
Let's make merry, our own shrine.
Cuddle close in the twilight glow,
With a wink, the fun will flow.

Mischief brewed in every nook,
With giggles echoing—come take a look.
We chase shadows, run wild and fast,
In this kingdom, joy will last.

The forest hums a jolly tune,
Underneath the laughing moon.
Branches sway to our silly grip,
Together, we're one wild trip.

Blossoms of Shared Journeys

In a crowded park, we share our snacks,
With crumbs flying like silly attack.
Laughter echoes through the trees,
Our friendship blooms with such great ease.

Silly tales of our past mishaps,
We giggle over tiny mishaps.
With each silly prank and goofy face,
Our hearts dance in this joyous space.

Like butterflies in a blooming field,
We spread our wings, never to yield.
In this garden of giggles and cheer,
Shared journeys blossom year after year.

The Lanterns of Loyalty

Under the stars, we tell our tales,
With glowing laughter that never pales.
Like lanterns bright in the night sky,
Our spirits soar, we giggle and sigh.

In the glow of moonlight, we swap our dreams,
Chasing fireflies, or so it seems.
Our jokes may tumble, but we don't mind,
Together we're silly, and perfectly aligned.

Through thick and thin, we share our snacks,
Mapping journeys on cosmic tracks.
Just like lanterns, we shine so bright,
A humorous bond, our joyful light.

Canopies and Connections

Beneath the trees, we play our games,
Silly nicknames, and wild claims.
With a canopy of leaves above,
We share our laughter, and endless love.

Hiding from the world's serious frown,
We create a circus, never a clown.
Jumping through puddles like playful frogs,
Turning our problems into silly logs.

With friendship as strong as the roots below,
We weather the storms, go with the flow.
In this haven of laughs and cheer,
Our connections grow stronger year by year.

Growing Together in Unity

In a world full of chaos, we stand as a team,
With laughter as fuel, we're living the dream.
Through hiccups and blunders, we find our way,
Growing together in the silliest sway.

Like vines intertwined, we twist and we turn,
For each silly lesson, there's more to learn.
With each goofy smile and playful jest,
We cultivate joy, and it feels like a quest.

So here's to the moments that make our hearts sing,
To the joyful times that friendship can bring.
With humor as our guide, let's keep rolling on,
In this garden of laughter, we'll flourish at dawn.

Treasures Beneath the Pines

Under pine trees, treasures hide,
Squirrels chasing, not a care in stride.
Acorns rolling, ants in a race,
Giggling branches, such a funny place.

Nature's gifts, we can't ignore,
Pine cones drop, they roll, they soar.
Laughter fills the forest air,
Finding wonders hidden there.

Nature's Kindred Spirits

Frogs in tuxedos, croaking delight,
Fireflies flash like stars in the night.
Trees whisper secrets, chatter away,
Creatures join in, ready to play.

Rabbits in bowties, dancing at dusk,
A bear with shades, oh what a husk!
Everyone's laughing, what a scene,
Nature's party, fit for a queen!

Whispers Among the Leaves

Leaves giggle softly, swaying with ease,
Telling tall tales, carried by breeze.
A chipmunk's joke, a lizard's grin,
In this leafy laughter, we all win.

Branches crack jokes, can you hear the fun?
Nature's comedians, with puns they run.
Heartfelt chuckles float through the air,
In this green laughter, no worries to share.

Evergreen Embrace

In evergreen arms, we laugh and spin,
A porcupine's costume? Where do we begin?
Hiding from bears, who think it's a game,
In this wild circus, we're all quite the same.

Jumping for joy, we swing from the vines,
Nature's own playground, with silly designs.
From the tallest treetops, the giggles cascade,
Forever in peals, we dance in the shade.

Trails of Togetherness

We wander in the woods, so silly and spry,
With pinecone hats and a humor that's shy.
Squirrels crack jokes, their tails like a flag,
As we trip on the roots, oh what a drag!

Laughter echoes through branches so high,
While acorns dance down like a pie in the sky.
Together we tumble, we snicker and roll,
Next time let's skip, for the sake of our soul!

The Mossy Path of Kinship

On a path made of moss, we giggle and squish,
Tripping on mushrooms, oh what a delish!
The owls hoot a tune, as we dance with delight,
In this silly forest, everything feels right.

We share sticky berries and start to complain,
Why do all tasty things look like they're slain?
With a whoop and a wink, we keep on our quest,
Navigating nature; it's truly the best!

A Love Letter to the Leaves

Dear leaves oh so green, your shuffle's a tease,
You whisper sweet nothings with each playful breeze.
I write you a letter, it's crinkled and fun,
Saying let's twirl around until day is done.

The giggles of nature are ripe in the air,
Each leaf has a secret, a quirk to share.
We tumble and glide, like children with glee,
Dear leaves, with you, I feel completely free!

The Air of Affection

In the air of affection, we float with a grin,
Counting the clouds as the giggles begin.
We hug every tree, like they've shared a joke,
A bark here and there, and we both start to choke!

The breeze plays a tune, our dance turns absurd,
As the butterflies chuckle, not a care for the bird.
With laughter as sprightly as the sun's golden hue,
Our hearts swell with joy, just me and you!

The Circle of the Elders

In a grove where the old trees sway,
The wise ones chuckle at kids' play.
Wrinkled bark, they can't keep a straight face,
With the wind tickling, they giggle in grace.

They tell tales of a squirrel's great leap,
And how acorns make the best food to keep.
With roots intertwined, they share a laugh,
Recounting mischief on the old forest path.

It's a raucous meeting of nature's own,
Where every wisecrack is generously sown.
Laughter echoes through branches so high,
As the acorns drop—oh my, oh my!

Each time the sun begins to set,
They spin new yarns, no sign of regret.
With giggles and gasps, their secrets unfurl,
In the circle of elders, life's a whirl.

Together Through the Seasons

In spring we'll dance with the blossoms bright,
We'll throw petals 'round and take flight.
With a hop and a skip, oh what a scene,
Chasing butterflies in the grass so green.

When summer comes, we'll swim in the sun,
Splashing and laughing—it's all just fun.
We'll set up camp with marshmallows near,
Telling tall tales, we have nothing to fear.

When autumn leaves fall, we'll rake them high,
And jump like fools, oh my, oh my!
Each crunch beneath shows our goofy delight,
As we sculpt silly shapes just for the sight.

Winter brings snowflakes, we bundle up tight,
Snowball fights waiting, oh what a sight!
Through all the seasons, our laughter rings true,
Together we shine, just me and you.

The Gathering of the Green

In the heart of the forest, a party erupts,
With veggies and fruits, all friends introduced.
The carrots conga, the peas do ballet,
While tomatoes giggle in a salsa sway.

A broccoli tree stands guard at the gate,
Hosting a feast, oh isn't it great?
They share silly stories, a root veggie mime,
With laughter and joy, they groove in their prime.

The herbs are wild, in a frenzy of sound,
With basil and mint spinning round and round.
The garlic bulbs sing out, "Let's have a ball!"
As everyone joins in, it's a riot for all.

When dusk settles in, the fun won't conclude,
With spuds doing impressions that leave us all mooed.
Gathered as greens, with smiles that glow,
In their veggie jubilee, they steal the show!

Roots of Resilience

Deep in the ground, where no one else sees,
The roots have a party 'neath the swaying trees.
They giggle and wiggle, tangled in fun,
While sharing their tales till the day is done.

With each little quake, they give a great cheer,
For bending but not breaking brings them such cheer.
They pass leafy jokes about storms and high winds,
In their underground club, where laughter begins.

Through drought and through rain, they hold their ground tight,
Spreading wise humor; nothing ever's too slight!
When saplings sprout, they cheer and they sway,
For resilience, they say, keeps the gloom far away.

So here's to the roots, so jolly and bright,
That wiggle and giggle through day and through night.
Let laughter like soil be the base of our range,
For in every small twist lies the joyful exchange.

Together Through the Seasons

In winter's chill, we start to race,
With snowballs flying, laughter's our base.
Spring brings flowers, we dance in the bloom,
But bees start buzzing, oh what a gloom!

Summer's sun turns us into fries,
We slip on slip 'n slides, oh how time flies!
Autumn leaves crunch, we jump and we cheer,
In every season, together we steer.

Embracing the Great Outdoors

Let's hike up hills, but wait, you stop!
Is that a squirrel or a furry mop?
With picnic baskets, sandwiches galore,
You drop yours first, now there's crumbs on the floor!

The campfire crackles, we roast some 'mallows,
You burn yours crisp, to our great, great shallows.
When stars twinkle, we dream loud and bright,
But who keeps snoring through the long, long night?

The Stillness of Solidarity

In silence we sit, oh what a sight,
Your snack bag crinkles, with a loud bite!
Meditating deep, we lose our zen fast,
As giggles erupt, a spell that won't last.

Together we fail at serene, steady moments,
You trip on your mat, how funny are commens!
Yet through all the chaos, we try and we grin,
In stillness of spirit, we find the joy within.

An Ode to Sacred Spaces

Our secret nook, where laughter rings,
Filled with treasures, and silly things.
You find a sock, well that's not mine,
Let's laugh it off, we're feeling just fine!

With candlelit talks, we share our dreams,
But your chair creaks loud, splitting at seams.
In this goofy corner, we feel so alive,
In every silly moment, our spirits thrive!

Conversations in the Shade

Under the broad leaves, we share our jokes,
The silliest tales spoken by leafy folks.
With whispers of wind, our laughter does blend,
Who knew that tree trunks could be such good friends?

Squirrels look on, their eyes wide with glee,
As we discuss things like what's for lunch, maybe.
We chuckle about branches that bend and sway,
And the time I mistook a twig for a tray.

Raccoons peek in, asking for snacks,
While we're busy sharing our leafy wise cracks.
A picnic of acorns, a feast full of cheer,
Who knew that shade could bring friends so near?

In the shade of the giants, life's never a bore,
With stories and laughter, we always want more.
As night falls with twinkles and stars start to gleam,
We whisper to roots about our secret dream.

Treehouse Companions

Up in our hideout, we rule the high ground,
With secret passwords that echo around.
Made of oak planks, our throne in the sky,
We're the kings of the branches, just you and I.

Plastic chairs wobble as we have our snack,
A feast fit for giants, a real tasty pack.
Peanut butter jars and jelly's our king,
In our treehouse castle, we laugh and we sing.

Cousins and neighbors peek through the leaves,
But only those brave get our silly reprieves.
A pulley of dreams lifts our hopes so high,
While we play pranks on the squirrels passing by.

With a fort made of dreams and laughter so loud,
We'll toast to the moments that make us so proud.
When the sun sets behind, and stars take their place,
We whisper our secrets in this treetop space.

The Flicker of Fireflies

As twilight settles and day starts to fade,
The dance of the lights brings a joyous parade.
Fireflies twirl like they're stars on a spree,
A dazzling show for my buddies and me.

We chase them around, with giggles and grins,
Trying to catch them, we're losing, but wins.
They blink and they flutter just out of our reach,
Wishing we had a firefly speech.

One says they're magic, all aglow as they dash,
The others insist it's just bugging out flash.
With each little flicker, our spirits do rise,
These glowing companions are clever in disguise.

Under the twilight, dreams do intertwine,
With each little sparkle, our hearts start to shine.
Every laugh echoes as cushions the night,
Together we bask in their whimsical light.

Sapling Secrets

In a patch of green, where young sprouts do grow,
We whisper our secrets, but only we know.
Branches are rusty, but dreams are so fresh,
For a duo like us, there's no need to mesh.

With mud on our shoes and leaves in our hair,
We plot our adventures with wonderful flair.
A kingdom of candy, where roots twist and twine,
In this magical woods, everything's fine.

We fashion our crowns from the soft, golden grass,
While critters look on and enjoy the sweet sass.
Sharing our secrets with bushes and boughs,
We laugh at the grown-ups and promise our vows.

When breezes blow soft and the sunlight is near,
We dance in our meadow, filled with no fear.
These sprigs of our youth will forever stand tall,
Bonded by laughter, we'll conquer it all.

Solace in the Green

In the park, we play and tease,
Chasing squirrels with knees like bees.
We'll never grow up, not one bit,
With grass stains and laughter, that's our wit.

Under trees, we spin and whirl,
Making jokes that make us twirl.
A picnic spread, oh what a sight,
We munch on snacks, till late in the night.

With every giggle and silly dance,
We find magic in every chance.
Nature's cheerleader, oh how they cheer,
In our own world, there's nothing to fear.

So here's to the fun, the friendship we share,
A bond so silly, without a care.
In the green, we create our bliss,
Forever in laughter, who could resist?

Navigating Together Through the Woods

Through twisted paths, we roam around,
Telling stories that astound.
With mismatched maps and giggles galore,
We tend to get lost, but crave more.

A squirrel stops, gives us a stare,
"Are you lost?" as if he cares.
We follow trails of whispers and fun,
Finding treasures under the sun.

With branches above and roots below,
We dance like leaves in a friendly flow.
Who needs a compass? Laughs will guide,
Through thick and thin, we abide.

When we trip, we laugh till we cry,
Falling's just part of the fun, oh my!
In every step, joy is our aim,
Navigating woods, it's never the same.

Embers of Connection

In the dusk, a fire glows bright,
Roasting marshmallows, what a sight!
We share our dreams, our jokes ignite,
With every laugh, the stars take flight.

A ghost story told, we shiver and squeal,
Is it spooky, or are we part of the deal?
With furry blankets and comfy spots,
Laughter dances, connecting us lots.

"Pass the graham crackers!" someone will shout,
Fighting over dessert, there's never a doubt!
With sticky fingers and faces aglow,
Embers of laughter hug us, oh so slow.

In this warm circle, our spirits align,
Moments like this are simply divine.
With every spark, our hearts intertwine,
Riding the waves of this friendship of mine.

Synergy of the Shadows

Under the moon, we cast our sights,
Playing with shadows, morphing delights.
With hands like puppets, we dance all night,
Creating legends, villains, and knights.

Around the campfire, we stretch and bend,
Our silly antics, they'll never end.
Every movement, a quirky pose,
In this dark play, anything goes!

Whispers of laughter fill the air,
As shadows twirl without a care.
The night is alive, and we rule the scene,
In this playful realm, we're crowned as the queen.

With every giggle and silly sound,
In shadows of fun, together we're found.
A light-hearted dance in silent delight,
Synergy blossoms, oh what a night!

Whispers in the Evergreen

In the forest, laughter rings,
Squirrels toss their acorn flings.
Trees giggle with the breeze,
Rustling leaves like whispered tease.

Mossy shoes and muddy socks,
Playing tag around the rocks.
Branches sway, a gentle push,
Every shadow's now a hush.

Woodpeckers drum a silly beat,
While chipmunks dance on tiny feet.
Beneath the sky, so blue and bright,
They share their secrets, pure delight.

Frolic under nature's smile,
Each twist and turn, a playful mile.
In the grove, so full of cheer,
Whispers echo, loud and clear.

Bonds Beneath the Canopy

Beneath the leaves, a merry band,
With goofy grins and outstretched hand.
Raccoons wear their masks with pride,
While the wise old owl turns aside.

Gather 'round for tales to spin,
As rabbits hop and owls grin.
Laughter echoes through the glade,
In this realm where jokes are made.

Frog croaks jokes that make us sigh,
While butterflies just flutter by.
Every creature joins the fun,
Chasing shadows till we're done.

As twilight falls, we share a laugh,
In this forest, we craft our path.
Beneath the stars, our hearts hold tight,
Bonds found here are pure delight.

Everlasting Under the Pines

Under pines, antics run wild,
Every critter, a giggling child.
Frogs leap in synchrony,
While fireflies shine like company.

Squirrels plan a nut parade,
In the shade, they plot and trade.
Pine cones fall with comical thuds,
Sending laughter through the buds.

Rabbits hop with joyful grace,
In this joyous, silly race.
Twigs snap under skittering paws,
Creating chuckles, endless applause.

When the moonlight starts to glow,
Friendship's warmth begins to flow.
In this haven, we all belong,
Under pines, we sing our song.

Roots of Kinship

Roots entwined beneath the earth,
Holding stories of our worth.
Laughing 'neath the arching boughs,
Nature's grin, we take our vows.

Chipmunks chatter, full of cheer,
While wise old trees lend an ear.
Tickling grass and dandelion,
In this joy, we are united,

Sketching paths with muddy toes,
Chasing each other, nobody knows.
Under the arch of leafy dreams,
The world is bursting at the seams.

From the roots, our spirits soar,
With giggles echoing, we explore.
In this forest, wild and free,
Unity's the best decree.

Whispers of the Wild

In the forest, creatures prance,
Squirrels hide, seeking their chance.
Birds gossip from branch to branch,
While raccoons throw a wild dance.

Laughter echoes through the trees,
Where bunnies bounce and do as they please.
A fox pulls pranks on sleepy bears,
While deer play tag without any cares.

Mice chuckle at the snorts of hogs,
In this wild world, no room for frogs.
Yet still everyone's having fun,
A party that's just begun!

When twilight falls, all gather 'round,
Sharing secrets, what a sound!
With whispers of joy, warm and bright,
Friendship glimmers in the night.

Whispers of Evergreen

Tall trees gossip with the breeze,
Whispering tales of ancient leaves.
A pinecone dreams of being a star,
While acorns giggle, dreaming afar.

The owls in night cloaks of grey,
Critique the squirrels, they've had their play.
Chipmunks chuckle with cheeks so round,
In this green maze, laughter abounds.

A raccoon sticks its snout with glee,
As the wise old owl calls, 'Look at me!'
Trees sway gently, sharing a joke,
Beneath the moon, they stifle their poke.

Evergreen friends, so silly and spry,
Watch the world scamper and fly.
In the timbered heights, 'tis a sight,
Their laughter echoes deep into the night.

Bonds in the Canopy

In the canopy, friends take flight,
Flying squirrels dash with delight.
Parrots squawk, "We're the best crew!"
While monkeys swing, just for a view.

Acrobats in the air above,
Chatting, giggling, laughing with love.
A toucan speaks with a beak so bright,
"Who's got the best snacks for tonight?"

The branches creak as they hold their games,
Hide and seek, exchanging names.
Not a care in this vibrant space,
Just trees and friends, in their happy place.

From the highest limbs, down to the ground,
Laughter sprouts all around.
Together they share, with joy and cheer,
The bonds here flourish, year after year.

Timeless Ties of the Forest

Within the woods, tied in mirth,
Leaves chuckle at their leafy birth.
A hedgehog spins tales of the past,
While beetles dance, moving so fast.

Every critter holds a story or two,
Badgers grump about the things they rue.
While fireflies blink some truths in light,
Shining bright in the starry night.

Their laughter flows like a gentle stream,
Unity woven, like a dream.
The forest whispers of tales once told,
Of friendships blooming, bright and bold.

In tangled roots where secrets lay,
They cherish moments in their play.
A timeless bond in this vibrant space,
In wild laughter, they find their place.

Stories Carved in Bark

In the woods where giggles spark,
We tell our tales, in light and dark.
Tree rings hold secrets, years gone past,
Echoes of laughter, forever vast.

A squirrel once stole my favorite snack,
I chased him down, but he had wings, lack!
In every crevice, a story's there,
Whispers of fun, floating in the air.

Adventure Awaits in the Grove

In the grove, we plot our quest,
With helmets made of oak, we're dressed.
Swinging on branches, we feel so free,
Racing the wind, just you and me.

But watch out for mud, it's a sly trap,
One slip, and you'll hear my laugh clap!
We tumble and roll, a splatter of glee,
Bobbling like acorns, wild as can be.

Secrets of the Twisting Trails

Down the twisting trails we roam,
With makeshift maps, we found our home.
The bushes whisper, "What's that sound?"
It's just a rabbit, jumping around!

But watch for the branches, they bite!
They often get me in the dead of night.
Through giggles, we stumble, never a bore,
Because every detour opens new doors!

A Cabin of Memories

In our cabin, we pile up dreams,
With marshmallow clouds and giggling streams.
Stories are told by the firelight's glow,
Of how you dared me to dance with a crow.

The walls are dotted with moods so bright,
From silly stunts that brought pure delight.
With every crackle, laughter ignites,
In this cozy space, we are free spirits' flights.

Unity in the Underbrush

In the thicket, we giggle loud,
Squirrels chatter, drawing a crowd.
A raccoon's dance makes us all grin,
As leaves whisper secrets in the wind.

Twirling in circles, we won't fall,
Building a fortress, oh what a ball!
With laughter echoing through the trees,
Adventures await with the buzzing bees.

Oh, the mischief we conjure each day,
With sticky paws, we'll giggle and play.
Our bond's a blend of laughter and cheer,
In this leafy realm, there's nothing to fear.

So come join the fun, don't be shy,
Together, we'll reach for the sky.
In the underbrush, we'll take our stand,
As a nutty crew, we're hand in hand.

Shadows of Companionship

When the sun dips low, we dance in dusk,
Beneath the stars, it's pure stardust.
With shadows stretching, our forms collide,
In silliness, we take great pride.

Jiggle and wiggle, an odd-looking crew,
The owl hoots loudly, "Who are you?"
"Just a bunch of pals under moonlight's glow,
Having a festival that's just for show!"

With the crickets' tune, we skip with glee,
Our shadows tall, wild, and free.
Laughter echoes, as we make our mark,
Bound by joy, we light up the dark.

As the stars begin to twinkle bright,
We find mischief, what a delightful sight!
With every giggle and playful tease,
In the night's embrace, we found our ease.

The Promise of the Pines

In a circle of laughter, under green spires,
We promise a pact, igniting our fires.
With cones for crowns, we wear our pride,
In this quirky realm, where fun won't hide.

A pine cone toss, who can throw far?
The laughter erupts, like a wild guitar.
With pranks and games, we fill the air,
In this shady nook, we've not a care.

The branches sway, bears can't quite find,
The secret to our, mischief entwined.
With whispered giggles, we chart our course,
In this land of green, we'll never feel forced.

When the sun sets low and shadows grow,
We gather our crew with a friendly glow.
Together forever, we make our vows,
In the promise of pines, we're silly as cows.

Symphony in the Silence

In the forest's hush, there's music to find,
A symphony plays for the silly and kind.
With rustling leaves and a babbling brook,
Our laughter dances, take a closer look!

A chipmunk serenades with a cheeky tune,
While frogs keep the time, oh what a boon!
Together we craft this joyous affair,
With hilarity woven in every layer.

The owls are laughing, can it be true?
In the silence, whispers of humor ensue.
Our frolicsome spirits soar up high,
As we twirl and spin 'neath the moonlit sky.

With a jig and a beat, we perfectly blend,
In this woodland choir, the laughter won't end.
Come join the rhythm, let's fill the air,
In the symphony's magic, we're a quirky pair.

Shadows of Loyalty

In the shade we gather near,
Whispers of joy and silly cheer.
Barking at squirrels, we chase and run,
Under the sun, we have our fun.

With tails wagging, we spin around,
In our world, laughter knows no bound.
Falling leaves become our toys,
Together we laugh, oh what joys!

Oh the games we play each day,
From hide and seek to a muddy fray.
With paws and claws, we'll play our part,
Bound by love, you've stole my heart.

So here's to us, the silly crew,
With every moment, our antics brew.
Under the trees, pledged is our glee,
Together forever, just you and me.

Leaves of Shared Laughter

In a pile of leaves, we leap and dive,
Each tumble makes our spirits thrive.
Squeals of delight, giggles in the air,
Every rustle sparks a joyful flare.

Furry friends with floppy ears,
Chasing each other, conquering fears.
Squirrels scatter, and we wiggle our tails,
Trading secrets in happy trails.

From dawn till dusk, our hijinks unfold,
With friendship's warmth, our stories told.
Marshmallow clouds and sunny skies,
Bumping snouts, oh how time flies!

So let's embrace this wacky dance,
With every bark, we take a chance.
In laughter's embrace, we'll never stray,
For in the leaves, we'll always play.

Roots Beneath the Surface

Beneath the ground, our roots entwine,
Hiding secrets, oh so divine.
Laughter echoes through the bark,
In every shadow, we leave our mark.

Paw prints scattered, zigzagging wide,
Exploring paths with tails held high.
Under blooms where giggles sprout,
We dig up joy without a doubt.

As long as grass grows beneath our feet,
Every moment shared is a tasty treat.
From bark to leaf, we weave a tale,
With each giggle, we shall prevail.

So here we stand, a goofy crew,
Rooted in fun like the morning dew.
Through every season, unshaken, we thrive,
In this silly dance, we come alive.

A Symphony of Needles

In whispers of pine, we take our stage,
Conducting giggles, this playful page.
Each needle falls like a ticklish plume,
　Together we twirl, dispelling gloom.

Harmony sways with our joyful barks,
Composing laughter in nature's parks.
　With every paw, a beat we define,
In this silly symphony, we brightly shine.

Oh the notes we hit, all out of tune,
As we dance 'neath the full moon.
Each misstep brings a gleeful cheer,
In this melody shared, I hold you dear.

So let's serenade the vibrant trees,
With our friendship's song that floats on the breeze.
In every laugh, a note we explore,
Together forever, who could ask for more?

Lifelines in the Glade

In the woods where giggles soar,
Trees swap stories, never a bore.
Squirrels tease, a chaotic race,
Nature's laughter finds its place.

From tree to tree, we leap and bound,
Accidental hugs are often found.
A branch slips, and we tumble too,
Rolling on leaves, oh what a view!

Bugs join in with a silly dance,
Twisting 'round in a comical trance.
The brook giggles, splashing along,
Making our woodland party song.

With every rustle and playful shout,
We cherish these moments, there's no doubt.
A friendship forged in the forest air,
Laughing together without a care.

Swaying with the Seasons

Autumn leaves in a silly swirl,
Dancing down for a leafy twirl.
Frogs croak jokes with amusing flair,
As pumpkins grin with a goofy stare.

Winter comes, snowflakes dive,
Snowball fights just to feel alive.
Icicles melt into silly drips,
We're rolling down hills with icy flips.

Springtime sprouts with a tender tease,
Buds burst open with giggles and ease.
Bees buzz in a zany quest,
Pollen party, it's simply the best!

Summer sun on our furry heads,
Laughter lingers in picnic spreads.
Swaying together, no one feels blue,
Through seasons we dance; that's what we do!

Intertwined in the Wilderness

In the tangled branches, we find our plot,
Adventure awaits in the silliest spot.
With vines like ribbons and leaves like hats,
We swing on branches, oh look at that!

The forest whispers with cheeky glee,
Mice pull pranks, oh can't you see?
They giggle as we tumble and trip,
Nature's antics—the ultimate trip.

Ducks quack jokes from their pondy throne,
Wily raccoons try to make it their own.
With laughter bubbling like a brook,
Each corner hides more than a look.

Together we play, in woodland cheer,
With every fool's cap, our laughter is clear.
Wrapped in nature, our spirits ignite,
Creating memories, oh what a sight!

Laughter Echoes Among the Boughs

In the canopy high, we share a chuckle,
Swinging like monkeys—a wild huddle.
Birds mimic our giggles with flair,
Singing along like they just don't care.

Bouncing squirrels crack a jest or two,
Their acrobatics—who knew they could do?
From branch to branch, they dart and dive,
Filling the air with their playful vibe.

Mushrooms pop up like little clowns,
Wobbling softly in their leafy gowns.
We join with smiles and shades of green,
Nature's own stand-up, quite the scene!

As the sun sets and the shadows creep,
Our laughter echoes—the memories we keep.
In the heart of the woods, bonds grow tight,
With giggles as our guiding light.

The Embrace of Bark

In a forest, we gather, cheeky delight,
Trees whisper secrets, hidden from sight.
Squirrels barter nuts, and owls crack a jest,
Life in the woods, oh, we are truly blessed!

With limbs intertwined, we dance in the breeze,
Branching out boldly, doing just as we please.
Saplings giggle as they stretch for the sun,
Laughing and bouncing, oh what fun we've begun!

Mushrooms peek out, curious and spry,
Cracking up branches with a gleam in their eye.
The fluttering leaves join in our silly spree,
What a spectacle, come laugh with me!

So here's to our laughter, our shade, and our light,
Together we flourish, and reach wondrous heights.
In this playful forest, with laughter so free,
Embraced by the bark, forever we'll be!

Heartwood Harmony

In the heart of the woods, where the sunshine is gold,
The trees share their tales, each one more bold.
With roots intertwined, we're a merry old crew,
Tickling the branches, just me and you!

A playful chipmunk, with a mischievous grin,
Darts through the shadows, let the laughter begin!
Logs hold our secrets, in rings they do tell,
Of joyful expeditions, oh, we know them well!

Under canopies, where the vines twist and twine,
We share all our giggles, our humor divine.
The breeze carries chuckles, through every tree,
We're rooted in friendship, wild and carefree!

So raise up your branches, let's sway to the tune,
Dance under the stars, 'neath the silvery moon.
In this whimsical grove, where the laughter's a spree,
Together forever, just you and me!

Forest Pathways of Togetherness

Strolling through forests, we take goofy strides,
With laughter that echoes, oh how it glides!
The footsteps of fungi, the giggles of fern,
In every nook hidden, there's a fun-filled turn!

A path made of giggles, lined with delight,
Every twist and turn, a surprising insight.
Branches overhead sway, they join in the cheer,
Nature's a party, come grab a cold beer!

With each bounce of the leaves, we play hide and seek,
The creatures all join in, as we laugh and we squeak.
A ruckus of root systems, a chorus of trees,
In this funny forest, we're quite at our ease!

So follow the trail, where the silliness flows,
In the nooks of the woods, friendship endlessly grows.
Together we'll wander, come relish the spree,
In this playful haven, just you and me!

From Seedling to Stalwart

From tiny acorns sprout, the stories to share,
Giggling as we grow, without a single care.
The saplings are staging a hilarious show,
With wigs made of moss, and roots in a row!

In the shade of our shelter, we chuckle and sway,
As squirrels crack jokes in their usual way.
The knots of our bark hold memories so dear,
Every ring tells a tale, as we gather near!

As seasons keep changing, we dance in the breeze,
With leaves that keep rustling, they join in with ease.
From mere seedlings sprouting to mighty and grand,
Our laughter's a chorus that echoes the land!

So here's to the moments, both silly and sweet,
Bound by our roots, we can't help but repeat.
In this whimsical world, where the fun's never far,
From seedling to stalwart, we shine like a star!

Reflections by the Stream

By the water's edge, we giggle and play,
Splashing around, just a hop and a sway.
A turtle looks on, with a grin on his shell,
Thinking our shenanigans might be quite swell.

We toss in some pebbles, the ripples expand,
While fish make a flight, a synchronized band.
With laughter that echoes, and a squirrel's cheer,
Nature's our stage, and we're the grown-up kids here.

The Dance of the Dappled Light

Sunlight is winking through leaves overhead,
Casting our shadows like dancers instead.
We twirl in the warmth, on this bright leafy floor,
A tango with twigs as we laugh, beg for more.

The breeze joins our party, a playful delight,
As bugs spin around in chaotic flight.
We pirouette past, with mischief we spark,
In this vibrant ballet, we're the kings of the park.

Among the Trees, We Thrive

We climb up high with a giggle and cheer,
The branches our stage, with nothing to fear.
A raccoon nearby, with a snack of his own,
Looks baffled at us, in our leafy throne.

The trunks tell our secrets, the squirrels they shout,
As each little critter joins in with a clout.
In the grand old forest, we make quite a crew,
Adventurers in mischief, just me and you!

The Forest's Heartbeat

With each thud of our feet, it echoes around,
The forest pulsates, in joy it resounds.
We leap over roots, and we giggle on trails,
As the shadows join in with our gusty exhales.

A fox gives a wink, and we wink back with glee,
In this wacky parade, we just let it be.
With chipmunks as cheerleaders, we storm through the glade,
In this whimsical world, our antics won't fade.

www.ingramcontent.com/pod-product-compliance
Lightning Source LLC
Chambersburg PA
CBHW070748220426
43209CB00083B/123